EGGSHELL
MOSAICS

EGGSHELL
MOSAICS

Gail Dziuba

Sterling Publishing Co., Inc. New York
A Sterling Chapelle Book

Chapelle, Ltd., Inc., P.O. Box 9252, Ogden, UT 84409
(801) 621-2777 • (801) 621-2788 Fax
e-mail: chapelle@chapelleltd.com
Web site: www.chapelleltd.com

A Red Lips 4 Courage book
Red Lips 4 Courage Communications, Inc.:
Eileen Cannon Paulin, Catherine Risling, Rebecca Ittner, Jayne Cosh
8502 E. Chapman Ave., 303
Orange, CA 92869
www.redlips4courage.com

Library of Congress Cataloging-in-Publication Data

Dziuba, Gail.
  Eggshell mosaics / Gail Dziuba.
      p. cm.
  Includes bibliographical references and index.
  ISBN 1-4027-2143-9 (alk. paper)
  1. Eggshell craft. 2. Egg decoration. 3. Mosaics. I. Title.

TT896.7.D95 2005
738.5'6–dc22

2005006522

10 9 8 7 6 5 4 3 2 1
Published by Sterling Publishing Co., Inc.
387 Park Avenue South, New York, NY 10016
©2005 By Gail Dziuba
Distributed in Canada by Sterling Publishing
c/o Canadian Manda Group, 165 Dufferin Street
Toronto, Ontario, Canada M6K 3H6
Distributed in Great Britain by Chrysalis Books Group PLC,
The Chrysalis Building,
Bramley Road, London W10 6SP, England
Distributed in Australia by Capricorn Link (Australia) Pty. Ltd.
P. O. Box 704, Windsor, NSW 2756, Australia
Printed and Bound in China
All Rights Reserved

Sterling ISBN 1-4027-2143-9

For information about custom editions, special sales, premium and corporate purchases, please contact Sterling Special Sales Department at (800) 805-5489 or e-mail specialsales@sterlingpub.com.

HAPPENSTANCE PERFECTED

On a trip to Rome one year I visited St. Peter's Basilica. Inside this magnificent church, I found art in every static form…except paint. Most walls are covered with mosaics, hundreds of thousands of ceramic tiles in every color and hue the mind can artfully juxtapose. The detail, scale, and proportion are truly staggering.

Photography of any kind is not allowed in most gallery areas of the Vatican complex, but it is permitted inside the Basilica. I thought that was unusual, assuming the art on the walls were frescos. Upon closer observation, I realized that all of the art in the church is either sculpture or tile mosaic. From as close as 20 feet, this incredible art appears to be achieved with paint. There is a luster, a glow that emanates from the walls. I was awestruck by the beauty, the detail, and the color variation.

Years later I dropped a brown egg and accidentally stepped on the shell. As the convex curve of the shell flattened, it formed an interesting pattern similar to a tile pattern, much like what I saw in the Basilica. I saved this eggshell and cleaned the remaining eggshells from that meal, then painted them blue, gray, and silver. I glued and affixed the shells to a small box in a series of squares to create an interesting textured pattern.

That was more than 10 years ago, and I haven't stopped experimenting since.

Projects may be a plain picture frame covered with small, delicate eggshells, painted to complement the colorful picture it holds, or a terra-cotta pot perfect for holding pencils, pens, brushes, soaps, or dried or silk flowers. Each project is personalized to reflect the hues of a particular room or the personality of a dear friend. And at the end of the project, the reward is a unique, one-of-a-kind creation.

Common, everyday items—a letter caddy, a purse, or a pair of candlesticks—can be transformed with a few eggs, paints, brushes, and decoupage medium. Look around your home; surely there is something there to transform with eggshell mosaics.

But first, you must break an egg.

Gail Dzuiba

TABLE OF CONTENTS

INTRODUCTION

Relaxation, whether by exercising or meditation, clears and frees the mind. Knitting, quilting, or putting together a puzzle are creative forms of meditation.

Eggshell mosaic is a cousin to these activities. Hands are busy and the mind is free to roam, plan, problem solve, dream, create. The best part is the cost is minimal and the results are great.

WHAT SURFACES WORK BEST?

Any flat or near-flat surface with a small amount of texture, or "tooth," can be egged. Slick, shiny surfaces, such as glass (A) and plastic, are more difficult. However, several projects in this book use glass and plastic that have been primed as a first step in the eggshell mosaic process.

Wooden items take the eggshell technique well. Wood can be raw (B), waxed, or already painted or stained (C). If wood is painted with enamel paint, simply lightly sand the area to be eggshelled. Metal surfaces can also be used—just sand lightly to give the surface some tooth. Papier-mâché items (D) are easy to work with and can be found in craft stores in a variety of shapes and sizes. Cardboard and heavy watercolor paper (140 pound or more) are ideal for smaller projects.

WHERE DO I BEGIN?

My favorite place to hunt for items destined for an eggshell transformation is a discount or dollar store. While the best surfaces are flat, you can work around curves, such as those found on a picture frame, by egging the flat portions then painting the angles and curves a complementary hue. The candlesticks in Chapter 5 are an example of this.

Craft stores carry many items found in this book, from papier-mâché boxes to small terra-cotta pots to pre-cut mats for picture frames. When working with a mat board, remember that eggshells will increase its thickness and may not fit when joined by the glass, so keep your eggshell mosaic as flat as possible or discard the glass altogether.

Wooden die cuts such as letters, holiday-themed cutouts, birdhouses, wooden animals, and plant picks are well adapted to this technique. Boxes in a variety of sizes and shapes can be found in lightweight wood or heavy paper.

Flea markets and tag and yard sales are wonderful places to find eggable items. An old purse with a great shape and sturdy construction takes on a whole new life with an eggshell makeover. An old, tattered leather letter caddy, personalized with eggshells, is useful and decorative.

One person's unwanted lamp and shade can become another's treasure after a good cleaning and a thoughtful arrangement of eggshells. Tables, painted and eggshelled, can add a real conversation piece to any room.

Before you take on an entire piece of furniture, start simple and small. After all, you're not eggshelling a basilica!

Materials List

- Acrylic paints, including metallic (A)
- Aleene's Paper Glaze
- All-purpose (tacky) white glue
- Awl or finishing nail
- Bamboo skewers
- Brushes: ½" bristle china, ¼" shader, No. 6 flat sable, small angle, thin liner (B)
- Cardboard or 140-pound watercolor paper
- Clear glaze spray finish
- Cuticle scissors (C)
- Decoupage medium
- Dimensional paint
- Eggs (chicken or duck, white, brown, blue, or green) (D)
- Emery board
- Extra-thick glaze sealer
- Floral wire
- High-gloss spray finish
- Jewelry hardware: pin backs, earring wires, posts or clips, jewelry wire, jump rings, jewelry pliers
- Kraft paper
- Pencil
- Scissors
- Sharp knife (E)

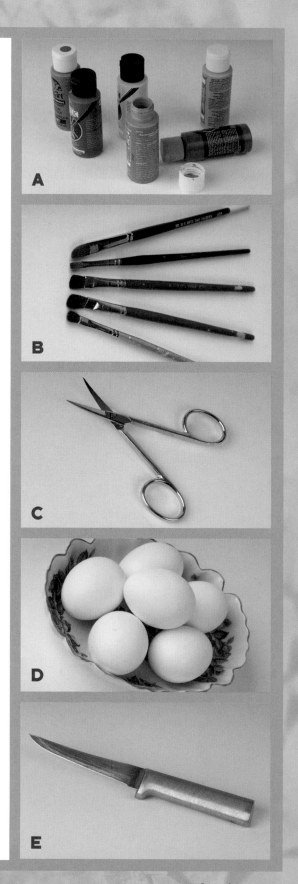

A

B

C

D

E

PREPARING THE EGG

Before you begin any preparation work, and start the process of eggshelling a project, be sure to cover your work surface with kraft paper.

All of the eggshells used in the projects throughout this book are painted and the paint allowed to dry completely before beginning the mosaic. For larger items, eggshells are broken in half and the halves are painted in one color or pattern. If flowers are used, for example, a half shell would be painted with flowers, the egg broken then arranged randomly to form the mosaic design.

Larger projects take many shells, which should be painted at the same time to stay consistent in scale of pattern and color. Many of the larger items, however, have been eggshelled with multi-colored and patterned shells. These leftover eggshells can be painted for a particular project, like the sports-themed accent table in Chapter 3.

To clean eggshells:

1. Crack egg in middle, leaving two pieces (A). (Using a sharp knife usually results in cleaner crack.) Reserve yolk and egg white for cooking. Rinse out eggshell with warm water.

2. Remove membrane attached to inside of eggshell by holding egg half in one hand and, with your finger, rubbing inside of the egg from the rim down to egg center (B).

3. Membrane will peel down and can be completely removed (C). Shell is now very fragile and should be handled with extra care (D).

4. Rinse with warm water and lay on paper towel, open end down, to air dry for about 5 minutes (E).

E

PAINTING EGGSHELLS

The versatile eggshell takes paint beautifully. Using a soft, flat sable brush (A), apply acrylic paint to the shell. Designs such as flowers, dots, lines, dashes, or swirls are applied by simply painting them on the shell surface. This can be done on a shell that has been basecoated or has not been painted at all.

Thinning the paint with water and using a light application can achieve a watercolor look (B). Allow the paint to drip and move on the eggshell (C). Salt sprinkled on the lightly painted egg will act as a resistant (D). The paint will move away from the salt, leaving interesting patterns. Inks and dyes can also be used.

The most important thing to remember is that before the eggshell is painted or decoupaged onto anything, it must be allowed to dry completely.

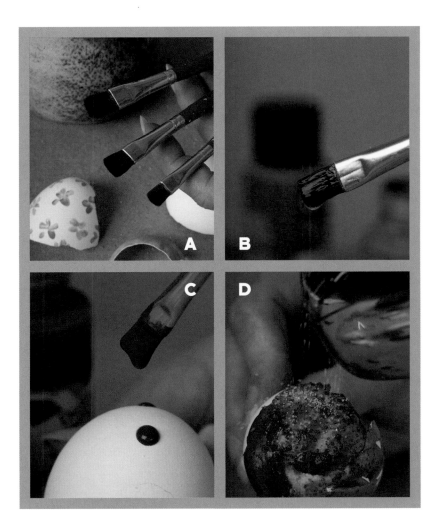

APPLICATION TECHNIQUES

It is easier to mosaic an item by eggshelling it in a random way. Because the decoupage medium (A) takes a few minutes to begin drying, work in a small area, apply only two or three eggshell pieces, then move to another area. This prevents disturbing the previous shells and allows for better distribution of light- and dark-painted shells. Apply eggshell to decoupaged area (B), then set in place by pressing down on eggshell, breaking into small pieces (C).

When using a variation of eggshells painted similar colors, or shells that are dark and light versions of the same hue, be sure to adhere the darker shells to the outer edges of the project to create a pronounced definition. Also, eggshells painted the same color but in different values give depth and dimension to the item, just as paint does to a flat canvas.

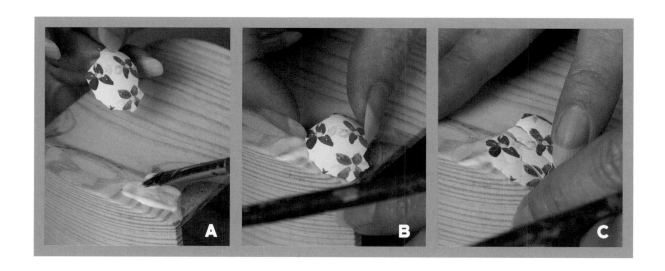

FINISHING TOUCHES

After each project has been eggshelled and allowed to dry completely, carefully trim any overhanging shells with cuticle scissors (A). An emery board can be used to lightly sand the edges (B). When the project is complete, a more finished look can be achieved by carefully painting the edges of the project with black paint. This covers any cardboard, watercolor paper, or eggshell that may be exposed along the edge after trimming and sanding. The black paint outlines the project and offers a more finished appearance.

If any shells break off, replace or reposition the eggshell and glue it down. Apply two or three coats of the finishing product chosen for the item. To prevent clouding, let project dry completely between each coat. Your creation will be sturdy, but not waterproof.

LEFTOVER EGGSHELLS

After most projects, chances are you will have leftover painted eggshells. It is a good idea to keep these pieces in a box for later use. An example of using these bits and pieces is the terra-cotta pots featured in Chapter 4. The lamp and shade in Chapter 3 were also started with bits and pieces.

The good news about multi-colored eggshelled items is that there is no wrong way to egg. It is important to place shells in a position that provides contrast and scale. This will be discussed in individual chapters on a project-by-project basis.

CHOOSING THE RIGHT PAPER WEIGHT

There are a number of paper weights and cardboard thicknesses available. The thicker the paper, the sturdier the project. When using paper, the larger the project, the heavier the paper should be. Watercolor paper is available at art supply stores and at most craft stores. The heaviest watercolor paper used in this book is 140-pound paper; anything heavier would be too difficult to cut into small shapes. Scrap cardboard can be used and is readily available by simply cutting a cereal box. Prime with several coats of acrylic paint to cover any printing on the project piece.

DIAMONDS

*may be a girl's best
friend, but eggshells are
certainly a lot more fun.
Jewelry can be
(clockwise from top left)
Art Deco, whimsical,
garden-themed,
or just plain fishy.*

Chapter 1

EGGABLE JEWELRY

I have a dear friend who would not consider leaving home without wearing jewelry, including a lapel pin. She has a large collection, from expensive to simply fun and whimsical. Having discovered that I could make pins using heavy watercolor paper, paint, and my eggshell method, I created a pin for her one spring. I designed a cheeky bunny peeking out of the broken egg. You'll find this whimsical pin, and other jewelry projects, in this chapter. A special occasion, celebration, or holiday can inspire a mosaic project. Pins are particularly adaptable and can be placed on hats, purses, and scarves. Designs can be adapted for the young or our most golden friends.

> ## JEWELRY PROJECTS
> *Jewelry Set, Red Lips Pin, Bead Necklace, Bunny Pin, Heart Pin, Flower Pin, Fish Pin*

JEWELRY SET

Materials

- Acrylic paint: black, metallic antique gold, metallic copper, metallic gold, white

- Aleene's Paper Glaze

- All-purpose white glue

- Awl or finishing nail

- Bamboo skewer

- Brush: No. 6 flat sable

- Cardboard or 140-pound watercolor paper

- Copper wire

- Cuticle scissors

- Decoupage medium

- Eggs: 1½ eggs will complete entire set

- Emery board

- Extra-thick glaze sealer

- Found objects: copper, glass, metal, and stone beads, gold disks, gold heart

- Jewelry items: 22-gauge copper jewelry wire, earring wires or backs, jump rings, pin backing

- Pencil

- Ruler

- Scissors

CREATE
a dashing set of matching pieces by using the same painted eggshells. Here, the base of each item is a heavy piece of cardboard.

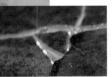

Instructions

LAPEL PIN

1. Measure 1½" square of watercolor paper and cut out. This is base of pin.

2. With awl or nail, make holes in three corners of square about ⅛" from edge of watercolor paper, then 1 hole between each (see Diagram A).

3. Paint front and back of pin base black; set aside to dry.

4. Paint ½ of eggshell gold, ½ of eggshell antique gold, and ½ of eggshell metallic copper; set aside to dry. This will provide enough eggshells for all four pieces in Jewelry Set.

5. Using bamboo skewer, dot white paint on antique gold paint; set aside to dry.

6. With pencil, lightly draw lines forming five sections on black-painted pin base (see Diagram A).

7. Gently crack eggshell painted with copper paint into smaller pieces. Try to provide eggshell piece with triangle shape that will fit into top space drawn. It is important sections of pin front remain defined. Do not let painted eggshells from one section invade another section.

8. Apply decoupage only to section of pin where copper shells are to be placed. Eggshells will not stick to any part of painted paper where there is no decoupage. If any of eggshells overlap into another section, simply break them off.

9. Break antique gold eggshell with white dots into smaller pieces, then apply decoupage in triangle section below copper eggshells. Lay down antique gold eggshell pieces.

10. Crack gold eggshell gently into smaller pieces. Apply decoupage to areas on each side of antique gold eggshells and lay in gold eggshells.

11. Finish eggshelling with copper-painted eggshell by breaking into smaller pieces, applying decoupage, and laying eggshells onto bottom section of pin.

12. Make sure small holes are still open and have not been egged over or glued shut by decoupage.

13. Set aside eggshell pin front; let dry completely, about 30 minutes.

14. Carefully trim any eggshells hanging over pin edges. Sand lightly with emery board.

15. Apply 2-3 coats of extra-thick glaze sealer to front of pin; let dry completely.

16. Cut 3" length of copper wire. Thread wire through side corner hole from front to back and secure by twisting wire around itself. String four glass beads and add gold ring.

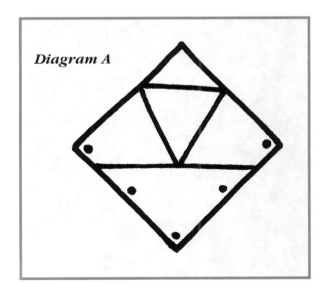

Diagram A

17. Reverse copper wire through four glass beads. Wrap wire end around wire directly above top bead; pinch off.

18. Repeat on opposite corner of pin.

19. Repeat process for two embellishments between corners and bottom, except string six glass beads on copper wire to add more length.

20. Repeat process for lower or bottom embellishment, using stone bead and gold heart for added interest.

21. Attach pin backing with white glue to back of pin; set aside to dry.

PENDANT

1. Measure 1½" square of watercolor paper; cut out.

2. With awl or nail, make holes in all four corners of painted square ⅛" from edge (see Diagram B).

3. Paint both sides black; set aside to dry.

4. Lightly draw in five sections used on pin.

5. Beginning at top of pendant, decoupage small triangle and apply copper eggshells.

6. Apply decoupage to section below copper eggshells and lay in antique gold eggshells with white dots.

7. Apply decoupage to two sides and adhere gold eggshells. Complete eggshell work on pendant with bottom section using copper painted shells.

8. Repeat Steps 14-20 of Lapel Pin.

9. Attach two jump rings to hole at top of pendant.

EARRINGS

1. Measure two triangles of watercolor paper 1 ¼" long and 1" wide at bottom (see Diagram C). Be sure to slightly square off top of triangle to provide more stability and surface for hole.

2. Paint front and back of both triangles black; set aside to dry.

3. With awl or nail, put three evenly spaced holes ⅛" from bottom edge. Make a fourth hole at top of earring triangle ⅛" from edge.

4. Attach copper, gold, and antique gold eggshells with decoupage in random fashion to earring front.

5. Repeat Steps 14-20 of Lapel Pin.

6. Attach earring wire to hole in earring tops.

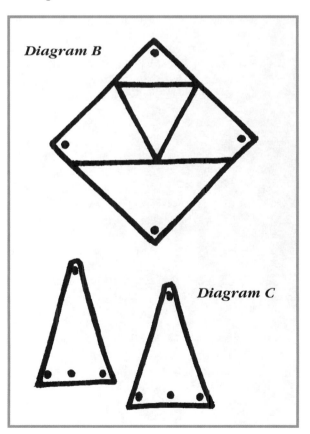

Diagram B

Diagram C

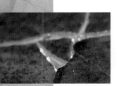

RED LIPS PIN

Materials

- Acrylic paint: black, red
- All-purpose white glue
- Brushes: No. 6 flat sable, thin liner
- Craft pearls
- Cuticle scissors
- Decoupage medium
- Eggs: 2
- Emery board
- Extra-thick glaze sealer
- Lipstick charm
- Pencil
- Pin backing
- Wooden square, 1½" x 1½"

Instructions

1. Paint both sides of wooden square black.
2. Paint 1 egg red; set aside to dry. Leave 2nd eggshell unpainted.
3. Lightly sketch lips on black wooden square.
4. Break red egg into smaller pieces and decoupage to inside of drawn lip area.
5. Attach unpainted eggshells to remaining area of wooden square front; allow all eggshells to dry.
6. Using liner brush and thinned black paint, carefully outline lips.
7. With cuticle scissors, trim away any shells hanging over edges. Lightly sand rough edges with emery board.
8. Carefully attach craft pearls to edge of pin with white glue, forming a "frame"; allow pearls to set and dry completely.
9. Apply 2-3 coats of extra-thick glaze sealer to entire pin surface.
10. When sealer has dried, attach pin backing and lipstick charm with white glue.

A PIN
*bearing a
company name
or logo makes a
thoughtful gift for a
business associate.*

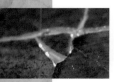

BEAD NECKLACE

Materials

- 1¼" wooden ball with hole
- 2" gold/brown tassel
- Acrylic paint: antique gold, dark turquoise, light turquoise, medium turquoise, metallic black
- All-purpose white glue
- Beads: 2 turquoise craft beads
- Brush: No. 6 flat sable
- Decoupage medium
- Eggs: 2½
- Extra-thick glaze sealer
- Ribbons: 1 yard black cord, 1 yard thin gold ribbon, 1 yard ½" lightweight gold ribbon

Instructions

1. Paint wooden ball metallic black.
2. Break eggs in half.
3. Paint ½ egg antique gold, ½ egg light turquoise, ½ egg medium turquoise, ½ egg dark turquoise, and ½ egg metallic black; set aside all eggs to dry. Break painted shells into smaller pieces.
4. Attach shells to wooden ball in random fashion with decoupage medium; let dry completely.
5. Apply 2 coats of extra-thick glaze sealer to adhered shells; set aside to dry.
6. Tie three ribbons together at one end.
7. String two turquoise beads onto thin gold ribbon.
8. Braid three ribbons together, adjusting beads approximately 3" on each side of center of completed braid. Tie off loose ends of ribbon.
9. Thread tassel loop through hole in wooden bead. Use white glue to secure top of tassel to bottom of eggshelled bead.
10. Place braided ribbons through tassel loop at top of eggshelled bead.

EGGSTRA HELP

MANY USES

A metal chain, a single cord, or just about any type of ribbon can be used to hang the pendant. Simply tie the two ends together to form the necklace. The necklace length is completely up to you. A beaded tassel can be used in place of a string tassel. Also, the same eggshelled wooden ball can be used as a lamp or light fixture pull.

PENDANTS can be hung from a delicate chain, ribbon, or a satin cord.

BUNNY PIN

Materials

- Acrylic paint: black, cream, green, lavender, pink, yellow
- All-purpose white glue
- Brushes: No. 6 flat sable, thin liner
- Cardstock or watercolor paper
- Cuticle scissors
- Decoupage medium
- Eggs: 1
- Emery board
- Extra-thick glaze sealer
- Pencil
- Pin backing
- Scissors

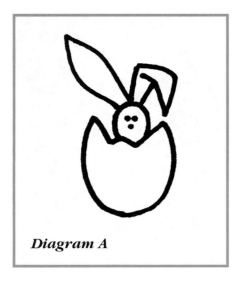

Diagram A

Instructions

1. To create pin backing, trace bunny on cardstock (see Diagram A); cut out.

2. Paint front and back of pin backing black; set aside to dry.

3. Break 1 egg in 5 pieces. Paint 4 of the 5 pieces cream, green, lavender, and yellow. Leave the fifth piece white.

4. Start eggshell application with bunny. Decoupage cream eggshells to bunny face and ears.

5. Add touches of pink paint to cream-painted shell; position to fit inside bunny ears and cheeks.

6. Decoupage white eggshells for egg portion of pin in random application. Decoupage lavender, yellow, and green eggshells on egg portion of pin.

7. After decoupaged eggshells are set and have dried, about 30 minutes, use liner brush to dot eyes and nose with thinned black paint. Draw thin lines for whiskers and to define ear folds.

8. Trim away any eggshells hanging over pin edges with cuticle scissors. Lightly sand rough edges with emery board.

9. Apply 2 coats of extra-thick glaze sealer; set aside to dry.

10. Attach pin backing to pin with white glue; set aside to dry.

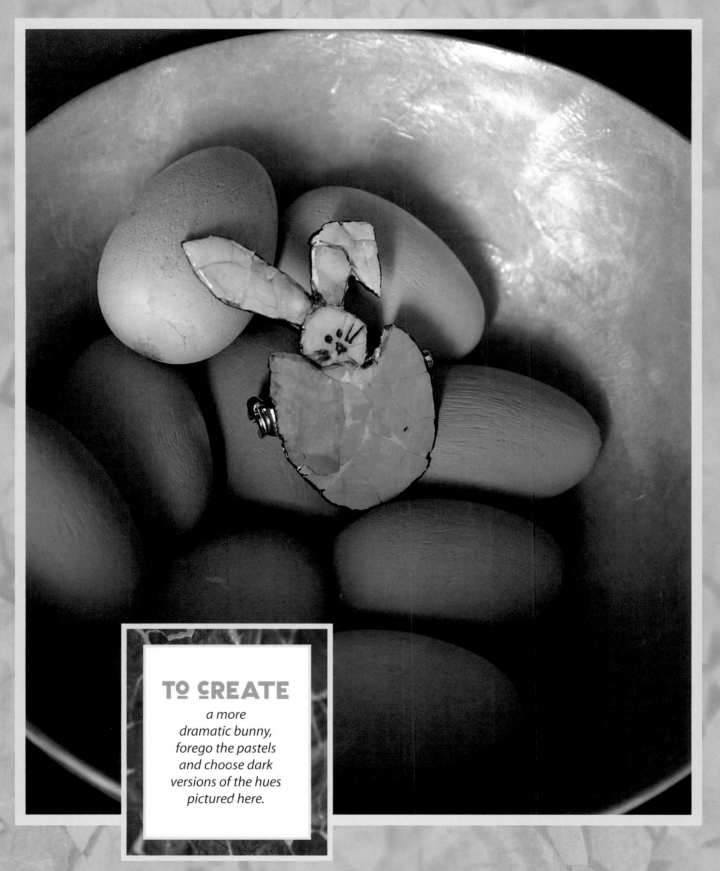

TO CREATE *a more dramatic bunny, forego the pastels and choose dark versions of the hues pictured here.*

HEART PIN

Materials

- Acrylic paint: black, clear bright red, dark barn red, medium rich red, white
- Aleene's Paper Glaze
- All-purpose white glue
- Brush: No. 6 flat sable
- Cuticle scissors
- Decoupage medium
- Eggs: 1
- Emery board
- Extra-thick glaze sealer
- Medium-weight cardboard
- Pencil
- Pin backing
- Scissors

Instructions

1. Trace heart on medium-weight cardboard (see Diagram A); cut out.

2. Paint eggshell using all three reds. Blend reds together on eggshell to create tone variation. Vary intensity of reds by using more or less paint on brush. After painting, set eggshell aside to dry.

3. With pencil, draw inner heart shape.

4. Paint inner heart shape and pin backing black; set aside to dry.

5. Paint outer area of heart white; set aside to dry.

6. Attach red shells with decoupage to white portion of cardboard heart; set aside to dry.

7. Using cuticle scissors, trim away any eggshells hanging over heart's outer edge. Sand rough edges with emery board.

8. Apply 1 coat of extra-thick glaze sealer to red eggshell part of pin only; set aside to dry completely.

9. With Aleene's Paper Glaze, fill in inner heart shape, allowing glaze to "pool." This will take a few hours to dry and harden.

10. Attach pin backing to heart pin with white glue.

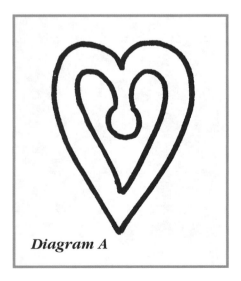

Diagram A

I WOULD LIKE TO BE YOUR GIRLIE.

PRACTICE
*your form
on a piece of paper
before you decide
on the perfect pattern
that's all heart.*

Chapter 1 Eggable Jewelry   **31**

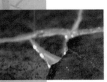

FLOWER PIN

Materials

- Acrylic paint: black, green, orange, white, yellow
- All-purpose white glue
- Brush: No. 6 flat sable
- Cuticle scissors
- Decoupage medium
- Eggs: 1
- Emery board
- Extra-thick glaze sealer
- Heavy cardboard
- Pencil
- Pin backing
- Scissors

Instructions

Note: When projects are completed, a more finished look is achieved by carefully painting the edges of the project with black paint. This covers any cardboard, watercolor paper, or eggshell that may be exposed along the edge after trimming and sanding. The black paint outlines the project.

1. Trace flower (Diagram A) and stem and leaf (Diagram B) on cardboard; cut out.
2. Paint ½ of egg yellow.
3. Paint ½ of egg green, leaving small portion of that shell to be painted orange; set aside to dry. Note: Adding white paint in small amounts to yellow gives depth to petals. Adding touches of yellow to green for leaves ties color scheme together.
4. Paint rest of green side orange.
5. Paint back and front of stem and leaf black; set aside to dry.
6. Paint flower face white; set aside to dry.
7. Beginning with stem and leaf, adhere painted green shells with decoupage.
8. Following curve of petals, adhere yellow shells to flower face. Add orange shells to center of flower; set aside to dry.
9. When two parts are completely dry, glue together with white glue.
10. With cuticle scissors, trim overhanging eggshells from edges. With emery board, lightly sand edges.
11. Apply 2 coats of extra-thick glaze sealer; set aside to dry.
12. Attach pin backing with white glue.

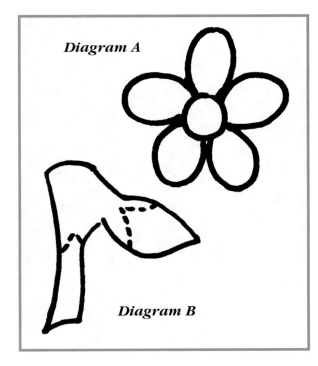

Diagram A

Diagram B

32   Eggable Jewelry **Chapter 1**

THIS FLOWER

*is sunny and bright,
yet a tulip or daisy
would look
just as lovely
on a lapel.*

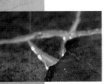

FISH PIN

Materials

- Acrylic paint: black, blue, gray, red, turquoise
- All-purpose white glue
- Brushes: No. 6 flat sable, thin liner
- Cardboard or 140-pound watercolor paper
- Cuticle scissors
- Decoupage medium
- Eggs: 2
- Emery board
- Extra-thick glaze sealer
- Pencil
- Pin backing
- Scissors

Instructions

1. Trace fish shape on cardboard or watercolor paper (see Diagram A); cut out.
2. Break eggs in half.
3. Paint ½ of egg blue, ½ of egg turquoise, ½ of egg gray, ½ of egg red.
4. Paint front and back of fish shape black.
5. Using decoupage medium, attach blue and turquoise shells to fish body and center of tail fin.
6. Attach gray eggshells to remaining fin areas.
7. Attach red eggshells to lips.
8. With thinned black paint and liner brush, paint fish eye, outline lips, and define fins.
9. Trim away any overhanging eggshells with cuticle scissors. Sand rough edges with emery board.
10. Apply 2 coats of extra-thick glaze sealer.
11. Attach pin backing with white glue.

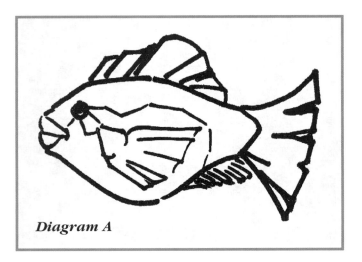

Diagram A

BE SURE to thin black paint before drawing the fish's outline by dipping liner brush and paint in water, then lightly wiping brush on paper towel.

WHETHER

embellished (clockwise from top left) with a monogram, a floral design, a face, or a black-and-white motif, papier-mâché boxes are easy surfaces to work eggshell magic.

Chapter 2
DECORATIVE BOXES

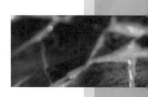

Small boxes can be decorative and useful. They can be used atop a desk, dresser, or vanity to hold paper clips, hairpins, pocket change, or just about any small treasures. Boxes can be eggshelled completely or shelled and painted. There are examples of both in this chapter. Ribbon, seashells, or lace can be added to any of these boxes to further enhance or customize the project. Look for sturdy boxes of wood or papier-mâché, and consider lining the inside of the box with a wonderful handmade paper, lightweight fabric, or even wallpaper. For a very dear friend or occasion, instead of gift wrap, a small gift can be tucked inside a box that has been eggshelled. Your special someone will know, without a doubt, how important he or she is in your life.

BOX PROJECTS
Book Box, Pill Box, Round Box, Star Box, Victorian Box

BOOK BOX

Materials

- Acrylic paint: basil green, camel, desert sun orange, gray green, metallic gold, red earth brown
- Aleene's Paper Glaze
- Book box
- Brush: No. 6 flat sable
- Cuticle scissors
- Decoupage medium
- Eggs: 5
- Emery board
- Extra-thick glaze sealer
- Lightweight paper (for spine and box lining)
- Pencil
- Scissors

Instructions

1. Paint 1 egg basil green, 1 egg camel, 1 egg desert sun orange, 1 egg gray green, and 1 egg red earth brown.

2. Paint box spine, back, and edges red earth brown. Paint "pages" metallic gold.

3. Trim paper to fit inside book box and on spine. Decoupage paper to inside of book box and on spine; set aside to dry.

4. Lightly pencil initial or letter to book box front.

5. Break 5 painted eggs into small pieces and decoupage to front of box in random color pattern. It is important shells do not cover initial. Allow eggshells to set and dry completely.

6. Trim away any eggshells hanging over the book box edge. Carefully sand edges with emery board.

7. Fill in initial on front of book box with Aleene's Paper Glaze. Allow glaze to fill in and pool in initial; let dry completely. Drying time: 3-4 hours.

8. Apply 1 coat of extra-thick glaze sealer to all outer surfaces of book box; set aside to dry.

AN EQUALLY *delightful alternative to this monogram is a family photo decoupaged onto the cover of this book box.*

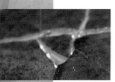

PILL BOX

Materials

- Acrylic paint: copper, turquoise
- All-purpose white glue
- Bamboo skewer
- Brush: No. 6 flat sable
- Decoupage medium
- Eggs: 1 brown
- Extra-thick glaze sealer
- Fabric or felt
- Ribbon: narrow, chocolate brown, 12"
- Scissors
- Small tin box

Instructions

1. Apply 1 coat of decoupage medium to top of tin; set aside to dry.

2. Using bamboo skewer, apply turquoise and copper dots to brown egg.

3. Beginning on sides then on top, decoupage eggshells to top of tin box; set aside to dry.

4. Coat with extra-thick glaze sealer.

5. With box closed, use decoupage medium to attach brown ribbon to outer edge of bottom of box.

6. Cut fabric or felt to fit inside tin box bottom and top. Glue in place, leaving top open until completely dry.

EGGSTRA HELP

A GOOD TRIM

It is important to trim fabric or felt away from the edges of the tin top. This will ensure that the pill box will close completely.

THIS PILL BOX *can be used for all sorts of small items like safety pins or sewing supplies, and can be easily tucked in a purse.*

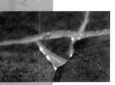

ROUND BOX

Materials

- Acrylic paint: beige, black, blue, earth brown, flesh, nutmeg brown, off-white, raw umber, red, soft pink, tan, white

- Bamboo skewer

- Box: 5" wooden round with detachable top

- Brushes: No. 6 flat sable, thin liner

- Decoupage medium

- Eggs: 6

- High-gloss spray finish

- Pencil

Instructions

Note: This wooden box is not primed or painted. Eggshells are adhered directly to raw wood to provide softer look to face.

1. Lightly draw face with pencil on box top (see Diagram A, page 44).

2. Break all eggs in half.

3. Paint 10 eggshell halves for face in four colors: flesh, off-white, soft pink, and tan.

4. Paint equal parts of remaining eggshells beige, blue, earth brown, nutmeg brown, raw umber, red, and white.

5. Fill in face with flesh, off-white, soft pink, and tan eggshells.

6. Apply beige, nutmeg brown, and raw umber shells to create shaded effect. For example, work on sides of nose with eggshells painted in darker face tones; these shells should also be used above eyelids and under eyebrows.

7. Fill in whites of eyes with white eggshells; nostrils with earth brown eggshells; iris' with blue eggshells; and lips with red eggshells.

8. Place off-white eggshell in thin area directly above eye, forming appearance of eyelid.

9. With thin liner brush and black paint, outline eye area and lips.

10. Apply pink shells on cheek areas and lightest pink eggshells on nose and area around lower lip.

11. With decoupage medium, apply red eggshells to lips.

Continued on page 44

AVOID applying eggshells under the lip of the lid or you will be unable to close this keepsake box.

Continued from page 42

12. Use lighter brown shells on top of head and darker shells on sides to create hair. Extend these brown shells down sides of box top.

13. Paint box base in rings using four of the colors in face—box bottom and first row is black; remaining three rows are browns, moving up from dark to light.

14. Paint off-white dots to separate bands of color on box with pointed end of bamboo skewer (refer to photo, page 43).

15. To eggshell sides of box, draw pencil line under top with top on. Do not shell area between pencil line and top edge or box lid will not fit.

16. Apply thin coat of high-gloss spray finish to outside of box and top.

17. Paint inside of box or decoupage layer of paper, stamps, or pictures.

Diagram A

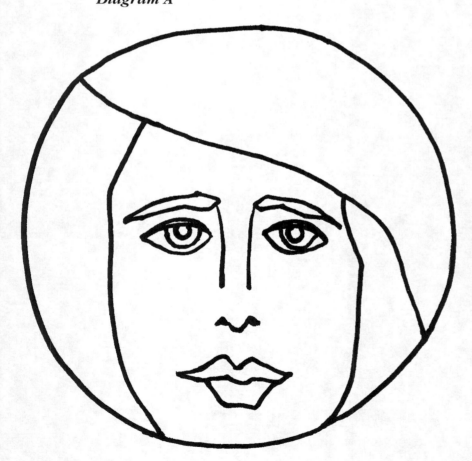

EGGSTRA HELP

PAINTING FACES

Some things to keep in mind when working on faces:

- *By studying your own complexion in a mirror, notice the darker and lighter areas. Use this study to help guide the shading of faces on a box.*

- *Adding lavender to any face color provides a shadow.*

- *Darker shells can be placed next to the hair and along the lower jaw area. Move around the face, using pink on the cheek areas and lightest shells on the nose and the area around the lower lip.*

- *Complete face with eyebrows, nostrils, and lips.*

Alternate Patterns

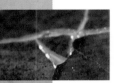

STAR BOX

Materials

- Acrylic paint: black, metallic silver, white
- Bamboo skewer
- Brush: No. 6 flat sable
- Decoupage medium
- Eggs: 1
- High-gloss spray finish

Instructions

1. Apply black and white paint in check pattern along top edge of star.

2. Paint sides of star, alternating black and white; set aside to dry.

3. Using bamboo skewer, alternate black and white dots (refer to photo, page 47); set aside to dry.

4. Paint entire egg metallic silver.

5. Decoupage eggshell in center of star.

6. Paint inside of box white; set aside to dry completely.

7. Apply 2-3 coats of high-gloss spray finish.

EGGSTRA HELP

INSIDER TIPS

In addition to paint, many different paper items can be used to line your boxes. To line the inside of a project with paper, trace box lid, sides, and base on paper and cut out. Using those measurements, draw the shape on paper and cut out. In addition to handmade paper, other materials that can be used to line the inside of a box include:

- *Favorite wrapping paper*
- *Lightweight fabric*
- *Photographs*
- *Postcards*
- *Restaurant menu*
- *Stamps*
- *Wallpaper*

A STAR *thoughtfully eggshelled is a gift itself and makes a wonderful jewelry box.*

VICTORIAN BOX

Materials

- 7" by 7" by 7" plain papier-mâché box
- Acrylic paint: black, dark green, lavender, light green, lilac, linen, purple, raw umber, white, yellow
- All-purpose white glue
- Bamboo skewer
- Brushes: No. 6 flat sable, shader, thin liner
- Buttons
- Clear glaze spray finish
- Decoupage medium
- Eggs: 1 (goose egg)
- Jute edging
- Lace
- Ribbon
- Scissors
- Scrapbook paper
- Thin satin cording

Instructions

1. Paint box and lid with linen paint; set aside to dry.
2. Trim scrapbook paper to fit four sides of box; glue in place.
3. Glue assortment of buttons, lace, ribbon, cording, and jute edging on corners of box.
4. Paint violas on intact goose egg; set aside to dry.
5. Crack goose egg in large pieces and position on center of box top, recreating intact egg. This will be like putting a puzzle together.
6. Decoupage goose eggshell pieces to box top.
7. Glue ribbon around side edges of box top.
8. Attach lace to top edges of box top.
9. After completely dry, fill in all areas of box top between goose eggshells and lace with white dots applied with bamboo skewer.
10. Apply light coat of clear glaze spray finish; let dry completely.
11. Add border of white dots on top and bottom of ribbon on top sides.

THIS VICTORIAN
box is ideal for stashing favorite greeting cards or treasured love letters.

HALF THE FUN *is finding the right piece to decoupage; the other half is watching its transformation.*

Chapter 3
FANCIFUL FURNITURE

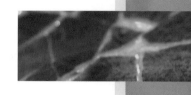

An oak table found at a hotel furniture liquidation shop was the first piece of furniture to receive a mosaic eggshell transformation. Although this is a larger project, the simple methods of smaller projects are the same—the project is done in blocks of colors. Tables in various sizes are available from a number of resources. Deep discount stores and yard sales usually have just the right piece that needs some special attention. These projects can be too large to mosaic completely, but will adapt very well to a combination of eggshells and paint application. It can be mostly about the eggshells, or the eggshells can be a wonderful, interesting accent to a painted piece. There are examples of both in this chapter.

FURNITURE PROJECTS
Sports-Themed Side Table, Accent Table, Telephone Stand, Lamp & Lampshade

SPORTS-THEMED SIDE TABLE

Materials

- Acrylic paint: 3 shades of brown for football, 3 shades of orange for basketball, beige, black, dark green, ecru, gold, light gray, medium gray for baseball, metallic gold, red, off-white, yellow

- Bamboo skewer

- Brushes: medium flat, No. 6 flat sable, thin liner

- Clear glaze spray finish

- Decoupage medium

- Eggs: 13

- Glass for tabletop

- Pencil

- Ruler

- Table with sturdy, flat surface

Instructions

1. Paint underside of table black.

2. With pencil and ruler, draw checkered pattern on table legs and border area of tabletop.

3. Paint tabletop black; let dry completely.

4. Draw in basketball, football, and baseball (see Diagram A, page 55).

5. Paint approximately 1 whole egg each off-white, light gray, beige, and medium gray for baseball. Principals of perspective apply in this application. Identify light source or direction. Use light-colored shells where light would strike object and dark-colored shells where there is less light striking object.

6. Paint 1 whole egg each light, medium, and dark orange, and golden brown and medium brown for the basketball. Yellow and golds can be added to orange to achieve tone differences.

7. Paint 4 whole eggs shades of brown, including grayed and very dark black-browns, for football. Off-white can be added to any brown to reflect brighter area of football.

8. Break all painted eggshells into smaller pieces after they have dried completely.

Continued on page 54

YOUR CHILDREN
may enjoy sports. But you may prefer gardening. Adapt your piece to the theme of your choice.

Continued from page 52

9. Using photo below as your guide, begin working around the design in small areas by first decoupaging eggshells to items that touch each other. Apply only 2-3 shells then move to another section, allowing shells to set.

10. Using dark green and gold, paint checkered pattern on table legs and border area of tabletop; let dry completely.

11. With bamboo skewer, outline dark green and gold checkered pattern on table legs with metallic gold painted dots to clean and sharpen lines between paint colors.

12. Apply clear glaze spray finish to entire table; let dry.

13. Set glass on tabletop.

Continued from page 52

EGGSTRA HELP

WORKING WITH LARGE PIECES

As with any multi-colored painted eggshell project, more eggshells may be needed. Paint additional eggshells in a variety of colors, using darks and lights, large and small designs. Contrast is important to the success of multi-colored eggshell mosaics. Paint as many shells as you think are needed at the same time so that color and application are consistent. If there are eggshells leftover from the project, store unused pieces in a box for use later.

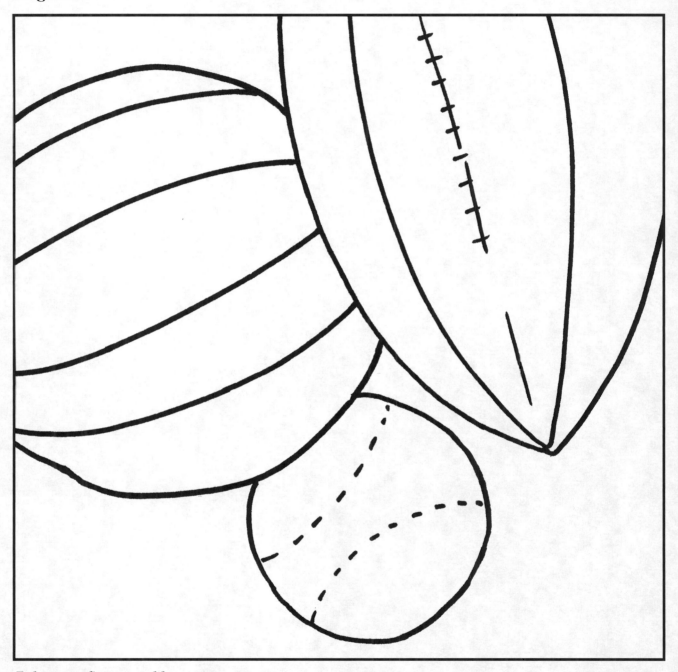

Enlarge to fit your table

ACCENT TABLE

Materials

- Acrylic paint: black, blue, green, pink, purple, red, white, yellow
- Bamboo skewer
- Brush: No. 6 flat sable
- Clear glaze spray finish
- Decoupage medium
- Eggs: 24
- Glass for tabletop
- Pencil
- Ruler
- Sandpaper
- Table with sturdy, flat surface

Instructions

1. Lightly sand and paint table white.

2. With pencil and ruler, lightly draw checkered pattern on legs and lip of tabletop. If table has lower shelf, any pattern can be decoupaged or shelf can be painted a solid complementary color.

3. Paint 4 eggs each blue, green, pink, purple, red, and yellow.

4. Begin eggshell application at outer corners of table. Decoupage eggshells in random way until tabletop is completely covered; let dry completely. Multi-painted eggshell mosaics provide contrast.

5. Paint black-and-white checks on tabletop edges and on table legs.

6. Using Diagram A (see page 59), paint medallion on bottom shelf.

7. Dot over edge of medallion with bamboo skewer and purple paint.

8. Apply 2-3 coats of clear glaze spray finish to entire table; let spray dry completely between applications.

9. Set glass top on tabletop.

If the table you are working on has two shelves, you can easily coordinate the colors of your eggshell mosaic on the bottom shelf. While you may want to eggshell the bottom shelf, consider a decorative pattern like the one provided (see Diagram A, page 59), or one of the Alternate Patterns on page 124. For a simpler option, pick up one of the colors in the mosaic and paint the entire shelf that color.

Diagram A

TELEPHONE STAND

Materials

- Acrylic paint: green, lavender, purple, white, yellow
- Brushes: No.6 flat sable, thin liner
- Clear glaze spray finish
- Decoupage medium
- Eggs: 6
- Lint-free cloth
- Sandpaper
- Telephone stand

Instructions

1. Wipe table clean and lightly sand any rough spots.

2. Using Diagram A, paint pansies on table in lavender, purple, white, and yellow, and paint leaves green.

3. Paint eggs in same colors used for pansies in random fashion. Paint some shells solid, some with dots, and others with swirls and small petals.

4. Decoupage shells in random application to top of stand.

5. Apply clear glaze spray finish to telephone stand.

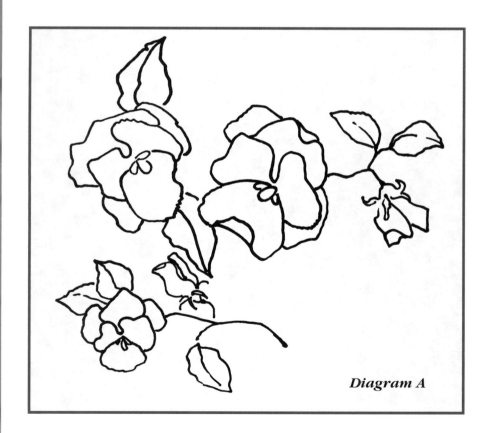

Diagram A

PAINTING EGGSHELLS *in the same color scheme as the pansies gives this telephone table uniform appeal.*

LAMP & LAMPSHADE

Materials

- Acrylic paint: blue, coral, green, lavender, orange, pink, red, white, yellow
- All-purpose white glue
- Bamboo skewer
- Brushes: ½" bristle china, No. 6 flat sable
- Cuticle scissors
- Decoupage medium
- Eggs: 36 (can use leftover eggshells from other projects)
- Extra-thick glaze sealer
- Feather boa, small
- Lamp and lampshade
- Scissors

Instructions

1. Paint all eggs even amounts of paint colors.
2. Separate painted shells into light and dark colors then small and large pieces (if using leftover shells).
3. Paint lamp base white.
4. Decoupage eggshells onto shade beginning at top; let dry completely.
5. With cuticle scissors, trim any eggshells hanging over edges.
6. Apply 2 coats of extra-thick glaze sealer to lampshade.
7. Cut feather boa in half; glue to top and bottom rim of shade.
8. Decoupage eggshells to desired sections of lamp base; set aside to dry.
9. Apply 2 coats of extra-thick glaze sealer to lamp base.

EGGSTRA HELP

WORKING WITH MULTIPLE COLORS

When creating a project with eggshells painted several different colors, keep painted eggshells in groups according to items in project. For example, group baseball shells together, basketball shells together, and football shells together. This organizational tip applies to any involved design. If there are shells with designs painted on them, select the main color in the design and group according to this color.

PURE FUN
*and fanciful,
beaded trim can be
used rather than a
boa for a slightly
different look.*

YOU NEED
only look outdoors to find inspiration for these colorful objects. (Clockwise from top left) A vase, flower pot, garden sign, and birdhouse borrow from Mother Nature's favorite hues.

Chapter 4

OUTDOOR INSPIRATIONS

Most of the projects in this chapter are small and relatively easy to complete. I've eggshelled dozens of terra-cotta pots and have given them as favors, thank-you gifts, going-away presents, and as seasonal accents for windowsills, desks, a kitchen, and bathroom counters. These special containers can hold pens, pencils, brushes, tableware, napkins, makeup brushes, or cotton balls. Three of the pots are decorated with multi-colored painted eggshells leftover from other projects. One pot is a mosaic with a distinct pattern and one is mosaic with a graphic design on its upper rim. The wooden birdhouse, chosen for its whimsical Victorian lines, was purchased at a craft store. Adapting it to the eggshell technique was a challenge, but not impossible.

INSPIRATION PROJECTS
Terra-Cotta Pots, Mosaic Flower Vase, Graphic Design Pot, Wooden Birdhouse, Garden Sign

TERRA-COTTA POTS

Materials

- Acrylic paint: blue, cream, dark green, gold, lavender, light green, off-white, orange, peach, pink, red, rust, white, yellow

- All-purpose white glue

- Bamboo skewer

- Brushes: ½" bristle china, No. 6 flat sable

- Clear glaze spray finish

- Cuticle scissors

- Decoupage medium

- Eggs: 36 (enough for all three pots)

- Emery board

- Lace, ribbon

- Lint-free cloth

- Terra-cotta pots

Instructions

1. Wipe clay dust from pots with damp cloth; set aside to dry completely.

2. Paint eggshells equal parts of all colors but white.

3. Decoupage painted eggshell pieces in random pattern beginning around upper rim of pots. Work down and around pot, using random shell application; let eggshells set and dry.

4. Trim away any eggshells hanging over edges with cuticle scissors. Sand rough edges with emery board.

5. Place white dots on pot lip with bamboo skewer.

6. Apply clear glaze spray finish to entire surface; set aside to dry.

7. Finish project by attaching ribbon or lace to top edge or lip of pot with white glue.

WHEN WORKING

with terra cotta, be sure to thoroughly wipe item with a lint-free cloth before adhering eggshells.

MOSAIC FLOWER VASE

Materials

- Acrylic paint: brown, cream, dark green, gold, light green, medium green, white, yellow

- All-purpose white glue

- Beads: brown and copper, small

- Brush: No. 6 flat sable

- Cuticle scissors

- Decoupage medium

- Eggs: 9

- Emery board

- Extra-thick glaze sealer

- Pencil

- Terra-cotta pot or clay vase

Instructions

1. Apply thin coat of white paint to outside of clay pot; set aside to dry.

2. With pencil, lightly sketch flowers, petals, and leaves (see Diagram A, page 70) on pot.

3. Break eggs in half.

4. Paint 4 eggshell halves gold, 4 eggshell halves yellow.

5. Paint 3 eggshell halves white, 3 eggshell halves cream.

6. Paint ½ eggshell light green, ½ eggshell medium green, ½ eggshell dark green.

7. Paint ½ eggshell brown; set aside all shells to dry.

8. Decoupage brown eggshells to flower centers and green eggshells to flower petals.

9. Decoupage white and cream eggshells to flower petals.

10. Decoupage remaining gold and yellow eggshells to pot in random pattern; let all eggshells dry completely.

11. Trim away any eggshells hanging over edges with cuticle scissors. Sand rough edges with emery board.

12. Apply 2 coats extra-thick glaze sealer to pot surface; set aside to dry completely.

13. Glue brown and copper beads to flower centers.

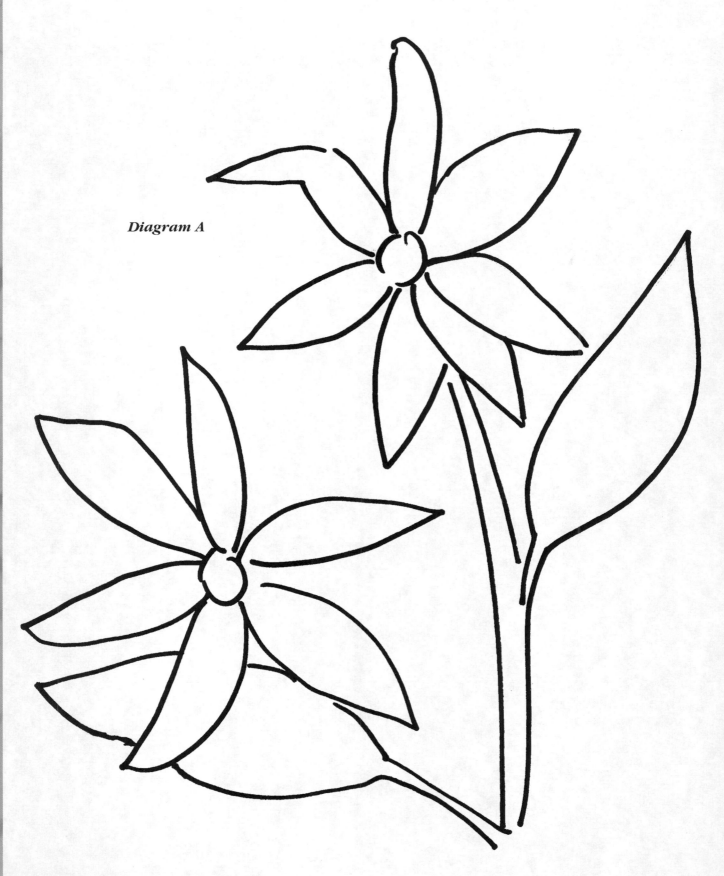

Diagram A

Alternate Patterns

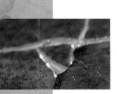

GRAPHIC DESIGN POT

Materials

- Acrylic paint: black, dark green, dark orange, gold, medium green, metallic antique gold, yellow

- Bamboo skewer

- Brushes: No. 6 flat sable, thin liner

- Clear glaze spray finish

- Decoupage medium

- Eggs: 16

- Lint-free cloth

- Pencil

- Terra-cotta pot

EGGSTRA HELP

TERRA-COTTA TIPS

When working with terra-cotta pots, remember:

- *If a clay pot or vase has a glaze finish on it, prep it by painting one coat of white acrylic paint on its surface.*

- *Terra-cotta pots with designs can be used; however, apply eggshells only to flat areas.*

- *Inside of any pot can be painted with acrylic paint or left in a natural state.*

- *Plants that require watering cannot be placed in eggshelled pot as the terra cotta will absorb water and loosen eggshells from its surface.*

Instructions

1. Wipe any clay dust from pot with damp cloth; set aside to dry completely.

2. With pencil, draw graphic design on pot (see Diagrams A and B, Page 74).

3. Paint surface of design black and rest of pot dark orange; set aside to dry.

4. Using pattern again, sketch in graphic sections in black painted areas.

5. Paint 4 eggs metallic antique gold.

6. Paint 2 eggs yellow.

7. Paint 2 eggs gold.

8. Paint 2 eggs medium green.

9. Paint 2 eggs dark green.

10. Paint 4 eggs dark orange; set aside all eggshells to dry.

11. Decoupage painted eggshells following provided color chart (see page 75); let dry completely.

12. Extend green sections along bottom of design by painting medium green curls.

13. With bamboo skewer dipped in black paint, dot terra-cotta pot immediately below lower edge of eggshell application and along sides of green curls; set aside to dry.

14. Apply 2 coats of clear glaze spray finish; set aside to dry.

SINCE rounded surfaces are more difficult to decoupage, you'll want to limit your design to the upper part of this pot.

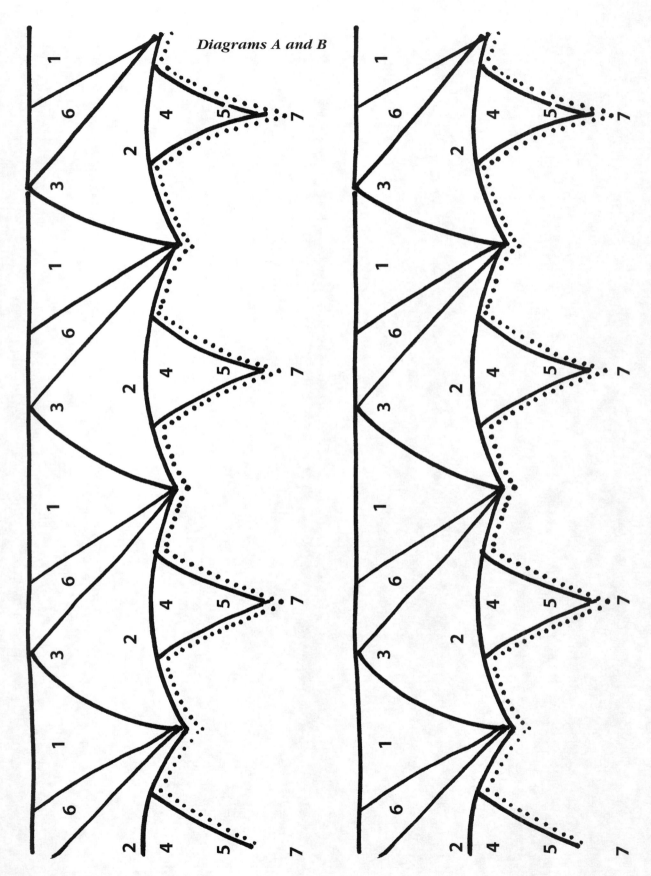

Diagrams A and B

GRAPHIC DESIGN POT
pages 72-74

1. Metallic antique gold
2. Gold
3. Yellow
4. Medium green
5. Dark green
6. Dark orange
7. Black (dots)

Alternate Patterns

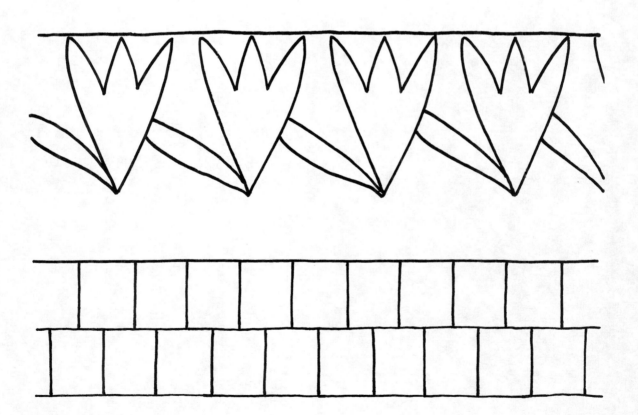

WOODEN BIRDHOUSE

Materials

- Acrylic paint: dark blue, light blue, medium blue, metallic gold, raw umber, white, yellow
- Bamboo skewers
- Birdhouse
- Brushes: No. 6 flat sable, thin liner
- Cuticle scissors
- Decoupage medium
- Dimensional paint: white
- Eggs: 6 brown, 10 white
- Emery board
- Extra-thick glaze sealer

Instructions

1. Paint entire birdhouse white; set aside to dry. Break 3 of white eggs in half.

2. Paint 3 white halves raw umber; set aside to dry.

3. Apply white dots with bamboo skewer to raw umber eggshells.

4. Paint 3 white halves light blue, medium blue, and dark blue. Apply blues in separate strokes that overlap but do not blend; let dry.

5. Apply white dots with bamboo skewer to mottled blue eggshells.

6. Paint light blue swirls on 1 white egg with thin liner brush.

7. Paint medium blue circles on remaining 6 white eggs and place yellow dot in center of each with bamboo skewer.

8. Apply dark blue dots around each circle; set aside to dry completely.

9. Beginning with hard-to-reach areas including eaves, posts, and front door, decoupage mottled blue eggshells to birdhouse.

10. Decoupage white eggshells with light blue swirls to front.

11. Decoupage white eggshells with blue circles to sides and back of birdhouse.

12. Decoupage raw umber shells to front overhang and chimney.

13. Decoupage brown eggshells to roof and base; set aside to dry completely.

14. Trim away eggshell pieces hanging over edges with cuticle scissors. Sand rough edges with emery board.

15. Paint chimney ornament in bands of metallic gold, light blue, and raw umber. Add white dots to chimney topper with bamboo skewer; set aside to dry.

16. Apply dimensional paint to eaves, ridges, and seams of birdhouse. When dry, apply 2 coats of extra-thick glaze sealer; set aside to dry completely.

INSIDE
OR OUT,
this birdhouse is
a heartwarming touch.
Unpainted birdhouses
are readily available
at craft stores.

GARDEN SIGN

Materials

- Acrylic paint: avocado, black, bright red, cadmium red, celery, cinnamon, clover, English ivy, light green, poppy red, raspberry, white, yellow
- Brushes: No. 6 flat sable, thin liner
- Decoupage medium
- Eggs: 9 white, 1 brown
- Extra-thick glaze sealer
- Pencil
- Plywood, 12" square, ½" thick
- Rasp
- Ruler
- Skill saw
- Wood glue
- Wooden stake (for stand)

Instructions

1. Using Diagram A (see page 81), lightly sketch flower, leaves, and bee on plywood.

2. Draw border approximately 1" on outside of flower and bee motif. Trim along outline with skill saw and sand rough edges with rasp.

3. Paint all areas of plywood that are background areas black. Paint back of sign black.

4. Break brown egg into smaller pieces and decoupage to stem of flower.

5. Paint 1 egg black, 1 egg yellow, and 1 egg with thinned black paint to create pale gray for wings.

6. Paint 1 egg light green, 1 egg avocado, ⅓ shell clover, ⅓ celery, and ⅓ ivy.

Continued on page 80

EGGSTRA HELP

MIX IT UP

A variety of colors is important for this type of project. Five greens and five reds were used on our garden sign. Any five different color variations will work.

BE SURE
to take your sign out of the garden during winter months to protect it from the elements.

Continued from page 78

7. Paint 1 egg bright red, 1 egg cadmium red, ⅓ egg poppy red, ⅓ egg raspberry, and ⅓ egg cinnamon; allow all shells to dry.

8. Beginning with leaves, attach green shells to leaf areas in random fashion.

9. Using same application, decoupage red shells to petal area of flower.

10. Beginning with bee's body, decoupage black eggshells. Save darkest or densest black eggshells for bee's head.

11. Adhere yellow eggshells to stripes on bee tail area.

12. Decoupage pale gray eggshells to create wings.

13. Decoupage darkest black eggshells to head and lighter pieces to eyes.

14. Using thin liner brush and thinned white paint, lightly draw antennae, legs, and mouth on bee.

15. Using thin liner brush and thinned black paint, lightly draw thin lines between eggshells of leaf to form veins and on flower to form petals; allow all paint to dry.

16. Apply 2 coats of extra-thick glaze sealer to entire garden sign.

17. Attach thin wooden stake to back of plywood with wood glue; allow to set and dry.

EGGSTRA HELP

MIX IT UP

Any flower of choice can be substituted, as well as a butterfly or a ladybug, in place of a bee. Remember, eggshell mosaic is not waterproof or weatherproof. If using outdoors, be sure the project is protected from rain or any harsh conditions.

Diagram A

GIVE A

(clockwise from top left) once-drab tray, bulletin board, candlestick, and frame a completely different look with dazzling eggshell designs.

Chapter 5
SIMPLE MAKEOVERS

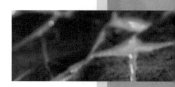

The projects in this chapter are all about looking for items around the home in need of a facelift. A candidate for eggshell mosaic can be purely functional or entirely decorative. Items can be shelled completely, or a combination of mosaics and paint can be used. Eggshells can give dimension to a design already in place in a room. Precious photographs in a mosaic frame, candlesticks embellished with paint and eggshells, or a useful tray can be a delightful gift or a valued possession. Consider applying eggshell mosaics to the sides and top of a tissue box. The design can be chosen to complement or blend with the color and style of a room.

MAKEOVER PROJECTS
Paper-Mâché Egg, Picture Frames, Message Board, Candlesticks, Tray

---

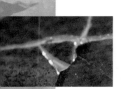

PAPIER-MÂCHÉ EGG

Materials

- Acrylic paint: light green, light pink, medium green, medium pink, rose, sunflower yellow
- Brushes: No. 6 flat sable, small angle, thin liner
- Decoupage medium
- Eggs: 10
- Extra-thick glaze sealer
- Papier-mâché egg, large

Instructions

1. With small angle brush and thin liner, paint 8 eggs using combinations of all colors with flowers, petals, leaves, and dots (see Alternate Patterns, page 71).

2. Break remaining 2 eggs into approximately 10 smaller pieces.

3. Paint 10 pieces with thinned green, pink, and yellow paint; set aside to dry.

4. Paint papier-mâché egg light pink; set aside to dry.

5. Break all eggshells into smaller pieces. Decoupage eggshells to papier-mâché egg.

6. After completely dry, apply 2 coats of extra-thick glaze sealer.

EGGSTRA HELP

EASTER DECOR

Smaller papier-mâché eggs can be eggshelled and displayed together in a basket filled with rye grass for a special Easter decoration.

WHAT BETTER *than an egg to eggshell mosaic? Small wooden or papier-mâché eggs bring wonderful springtime charm.*

PASTEL FLOWER FRAME

Materials

- Acrylic paint: black, blush, coral, light green, medium green, peach, pink, white
- Brush: No. 6 flat sable
- Cuticle scissors
- Decoupage medium
- Eggs: 8
- Emery board
- Extra-thick glaze sealer
- Frame

Instructions

1. Prime frame with white paint.
2. Paint 8 eggs in floral motif, swirls, dots, and leaves (see Alternate Patterns, page 71).
3. Decoupage shells on sides of frame in random fashion.
4. Decoupage eggshells to front of frame in random fashion; let dry.
5. With cuticle scissors, trim away any shells hanging over edges of project. Lightly sand rough edges with emery board.
6. Apply 2 coats of extra-thick glaze sealer.

EGGSTRA HELP

WORKING WITH FRAMES

When selecting a frame to eggshell, keep in mind the following:

- *Frames that have flat surfaces work best. Curves and slopes are more difficult to mosaic.*
- *Choosing a color or tone in your photograph will best enhance its frame.*
- *Black frames add drama to many photographs.*
- *Stylized pink flowers may be added to soften and accent the frame.*

A COLOR SCHEME *that is monochromatic or pastels is perfect for an eggshell frame that holds a black-and-white photo of a loved one.*

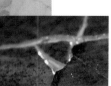

MESSAGE BOARD

Materials

- Acrylic paint: black, burnt sienna, coral, cream, light yellow, peach, white

- Brushes: ½" bristle china, No. 6 flat sable, thin liner

- Decoupage medium

- Eggs: 3

- Extra-thick glaze sealer

- Message board

- Pencil

- Ruler

Instructions

1. Prime message board frame with white paint; set aside to dry.

2. Using ruler, line off squares on frame.

3. Sketch fish on board with pencil (see Diagram A).

4. Paint message board light yellow.

5. Paint black stripes on frame.

6. Using coral paint, block in fish.

7. Paint fish scales cream and burnt sienna; let all painted surfaces dry completely.

8. Paint 1 egg burnt sienna.

9. Paint 1 egg coral.

10. Paint ½ egg peach, ½ egg cream; set aside to dry completely.

11. Decoupage eggshells to fish back, fins, scales, and tip of tail; set aside to dry.

12. With thin liner brush and thinned black paint, draw line around scales, accent tail, gills, and bottom jaw.

13. Paint in white fish eye and black pupil with bristle china brush. Line white fish eye with thinned black paint; set aside to dry completely.

14. Apply 2 coats of extra-thick glaze sealer.

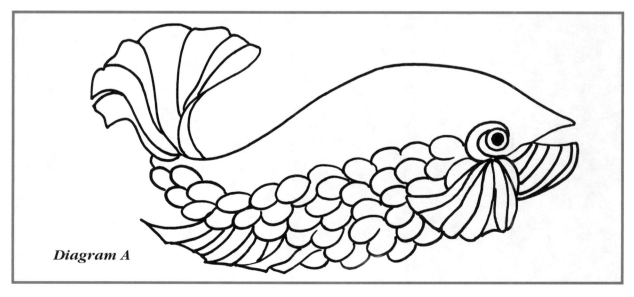

Diagram A

WHILE a fish looks great in a nautical-inspired kitchen, a bowl of fruit or vegetables is just as lovely.

BLACK PICTURE FRAME

Materials

- Acrylic paint: black, blush, coral, pink, white
- All-purpose white glue
- Bamboo skewer
- Brush: No. 6 flat sable
- Cuticle scissors
- Decoupage medium
- Eggs: 8
- Emery board
- Extra-thick glaze sealer
- Frame
- Small white pearls

Instructions

1. Prime frame with white acrylic paint.
2. Paint 6 eggshells black; set aside to dry.
3. Using bamboo skewer and white paint, dot black shells; set aside to dry.
4. Paint 1 egg coral; set aside to dry.
5. Paint ½ egg pink; set aside to dry.
6. Paint ½ egg blush; set aside to dry.
7. Decoupage black eggshells over entire frame; set aside to dry.
8. Attach 4 small pieces of coral shell on top of black shells to form flower petals; set aside to dry.
9. Attach 3 small pieces of pink shell on top of coral shells to form second row of petals; allow to set.
10. Attach 2 small pieces of blush shell on top of pink shells to form third layer of petals. This will result in dimensional pink flower.
11. Attach white pearl to center of pink flower with white glue; set aside to dry completely.
12. Apply 2 coats of extra-thick glaze sealer.

BLACK-PAINTED *eggshells lend a project high drama, especially when married with a lighter accent like these flowers.*

CANDLESTICKS

Materials

- Acrylic paint: beige, black, coral, dark green, medium green, melon, raw umber, white

- Bamboo skewers

- Brushes: ¼" shader, No. 6 flat sable, thin liner

- Candlesticks

- Decoupage medium

- Eggs: 2

- Extra-thick glaze sealer

- Pencil

- Ruler

Instructions

1. Using pencil and ruler, mark off checks on candlestick base.

2. Beginning at base, paint black-and-white checks.

3. With thin liner brush, paint 1 egg with coral and melon floral motifs.

4. Paint ½ egg raw umber with sable brush.

5. Paint ½ egg with medium green swirl using thin liner brush.

6. Moving up candlestick, paint band of cream then dot with raw umber using bamboo skewer.

7. Apply heavy coat of raw umber to next band. Dot with white paint and bamboo skewer.

8. Add white paint to coral to create light coral band.

9. Dot edges of coral band with beige paint and bamboo skewer.

10. Decoupage painted eggshells in random pattern to next band.

11. Paint next band beige; dot with white paint and bamboo skewer.

12. Paint next band dark green; dot with medium green paint and bamboo skewer.

13. Paint thin band of medium green; dot with dark green paint and bamboo skewer.

Continued on page 94

MIXING *and matching your colors and techniques is a whimsical approach to a candlestick makeover. Just remember to let each part dry before moving on to the next section.*

Continued from page 92

14. Paint body of candlestick beige; dot with white paint in looping pattern and bamboo skewer.

15. Decoupage painted eggshells in random application to next band.

16. Paint next band melon; dot with coral paint and bamboo skewer.

17. Paint next band coral; dot with medium green paint and bamboo skewer and paint center white.

18. Paint raw umber band and accent with white floral motif.

19. Repeat coral band; dot with medium green paint and bamboo skewer and paint center white.

20. Repeat melon band with coral dots.

21. Decoupage painted eggshells in random application to next band.

22. Paint raw umber under upper lip of candlestick; dot with medium green paint and bamboo skewer.

23. Paint next band medium green.

24. Alternate beige and coral checks on top of lip.

25. Dot with white and black paint and bamboo skewer.

26. Paint candlestick top beige; dot with white paint and bamboo skewer.

27. Let candlestick dry completely.

28. Apply 2 coats of extra-thick glaze sealer.

EGGSTRA HELP

COLOR SIMPLIFIED

While this project has many steps, it is easy to accomplish. The band-by-band coloration can be applied to any cylinder item and accented with an occasional mosaic application. Simplify a complicated color scheme by painting larger areas in only one color. Decorate larger color bands with dots and floral motifs.

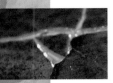

TRAY

Materials

- Acrylic paint: black, gold, lavender, light blue, light green, medium green, plum, white, yellow
- Bamboo skewer
- Brushes: ¼" shader, ½" bristle china, No. 6 flat sable
- Clear glaze spray finish
- Cuticle scissors
- Decoupage medium
- Eggs: 16
- Emery board
- Pencil
- Ruler
- Tray

Instructions

1. Paint interior and exterior sides and bottom of tray black; set aside to dry.
2. Draw crocus design around inside of tray to form border (see Diagrams A and B, page 99).
3. Paint inside of tray light green background.
4. Paint circles gold.
5. Paint petals light blue.
6. Paint yellow centers; add ring of white dots with bamboo skewer.
7. Paint crocus petals lavender and plum.
8. Paint stems and long leaves medium green.
9. Paint all eggs black; set aside to dry.
10. Using ruler and pencil, line off checks on tray rim and across handles.
11. Paint white stripes around top of tray sides and handle.
12. Apply 1 coat of clear glaze spray finish.
13. Decoupage eggshells to sides of tray; set aside to dry completely.
14. With cuticle scissors, trim away any eggshells hanging over edges. Lightly sand rough edges with emery board.
15. Apply 2 coats of clear glaze spray finish to entire tray; set aside to dry completely.

BREAKFAST *is served on a crocus-painted tray seemingly fresh from the garden.*

BLACK
PAINTED
*eggshells give this tray
an artfully aged
appearance.*

TRAY TIPS

When working with a tray, some things to keep in mind:

- *The inside of a tray can be painted a solid color or decoupaged with favorite pictures, napkins, travel brochures, or matchbook covers.*

- *Glass cut to fit a tray will protect the interior tray surface. Plexiglas is a lightweight alternative but is easily scratched.*

- *Silicone sealer can be used to hold glass or plexiglas in place and also keeps moisture from reaching tray surface. Just remember, silicone is permanent.*

- *Clean tray with damp cloth only.*

Diagrams A and B

IF IT'S STURDY, *it can be eggshelled. (Clockwise from top left) An old purse, a rabbit pick, a letter caddy, and a gift tag meet this requirement.*

Chapter 6

GIFT PROJECTS

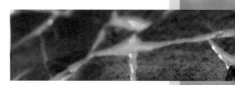

The projects in this chapter are unrelated except that they developed unexpectedly. When shopping for objects to eggshell mosaic, keep an open mind and a keen eye. Think outside of the box. Look for things that are sturdy, have flat or nearly flat surfaces, are either useful or have attitude, have good bones or an interesting shape, and even items in need of a facelift. A plain journal can be eggshelled with an initial on the cover. Or, consider a drab hand-held mirror that has great possibility. Stroll through your favorite dollar store or discount outlet for small items waiting for a new look. Just be sure to clean your items thoroughly before beginning the eggshell mosaic process. The perfect eggshell mosaic item is just waiting to be discovered.

GIFT PROJECTS
Purse, Gift Box Decorations, Rabbit Pick, Leather Letter Caddy

EVERYDAY PURSE

Materials

- Acrylic paint: blue, green, pink, yellow, white

- Bamboo skewer

- Brush: No. 6 flat sable

- Clear glaze spray finish

- Cuticle scissors

- Decoupage medium

- Eggs: 24

- Emery board

- Lint-free cloth

- Purse

Instructions

1. Clean purse with damp cloth; set aside to dry.

2. Paint 6 eggs blue, 6 eggs green, 6 eggs pink, 6 eggs yellow; set aside to dry.

3. Using bamboo skewer and white paint, apply white dots to painted eggshells.

4. Beginning in cracks, crevices, and hard-to-reach areas of purse, decoupage painted eggshells in random fashion. Do not eggshell bottom of purse.

5. With cuticle scissors, trim away any eggshells hanging over edges. Lightly sand rough edges with emery board.

6. Apply 2-3 coats of clear glaze spray finish.

Note: *Once eggshells are decoupaged in place and have dried, they will not come off unless project becomes wet and is allowed to stay wet.*

SINCE
a purse typically undergoes a great amount of wear, avoid eggshelling its bottom surface.

BABY RATTLE

Materials

- Acrylic paint: pink, white
- Bamboo skewers
- Brush: No. 6 flat sable
- Cuticle scissors
- Decoupage medium
- Eggs: 2
- Emery board
- Extra-thick glaze sealer
- Ribbon
- Thin felt tip pen
- Wooden die cut: baby rattle with heart

Instructions

1. Prime die cut with white paint.
2. Paint 2 eggs pink; set aside to dry.
3. Decoupage eggshells to die cut; set aside to dry.
4. With cuticle scissors, trim away any shells hanging over edges of die cut. Sand rough edges with emery board.
5. Paint edges and back of die cut pink; set aside to dry.
6. Using bamboo skewer, apply white dots to edges of rattle; set aside to dry.
7. Paint heart portion of rattle white; set aside to dry.
8. Using bamboo skewer, apply pink and white dots to heart; set aside to dry.
9. Write recipient's name and date of occasion on back.
10. Apply 2 coats of extra-thick glaze sealer.
11. Tie on ribbon and attach to gift.

WHILE this rattle is pretty in pink, it would be just as sweet in boy blue. Consider tying it to a baby shower gift.

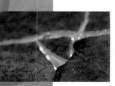

LUGGAGE TAG

Materials

- Acrylic paint: brown, cream, green, taupe
- Bamboo skewer
- Brush: No. 6 flat sable
- Cuticle scissors
- Decoupage medium
- Eggs: 2
- Emery board
- Extra-thick glaze sealer
- Ribbon
- Thin felt tip pen
- Wooden die cut: luggage tag

Instructions

1. Prime wooden die cut with brown paint.
2. Break eggs into halves.
3. Paint ½ egg taupe, ½ egg brown, ½ egg green, ½ egg cream.
4. Decoupage painted eggshells in random application on die cut.
5. Using cuticle scissors, trim away any eggshells hanging over edges. Sand rough edges with emery board.
6. Finish back of tag with taupe paint or decoupage with decorative paper.
7. Write name of recipient and date on back.
8. Apply 2-3 coats of extra-thick glaze sealer.
9. Tie luggage tag to ribbon and attach to gift package.

EGGSTRA HELP

USING WOODEN ACCENTS

Any wooden die cut can add a special touch to a wrapped gift. If a hole is needed in the die cut, place masking tape on area where hole is desired. Gently hammer a finishing nail through masking tape and wood before beginning the project. Be sure the hole remains open while working on the project. Also, do not eggshell the bottom of items to be placed on a wooden surface. Even with 2-3 finish coats on the project, wooden surfaces can become scratched.

PURELY *decorative and ideal for a bon voyage gift, this luggage tag can be added to a memory album long after the return home.*

RABBIT PICK

Materials

- Acrylic paint: beige, brown, cream, off-white, pink, taupe
- Brush: No. 6 flat sable
- Cuticle scissors
- Decoupage medium
- Eggs: 3
- Emery board
- Extra-thick glaze sealer
- Wooden die cut: rabbit pick

Instructions

1. Prime die cut with brown paint.

2. Break eggs into halves.

3. Paint ½ egg pink, ½ egg off-white, ½ egg taupe, ½ egg beige, ½ egg cream; leave ½ egg unpainted.

4. Decoupage pink eggshells on ears and area of mouth, darker shells in area between front legs and bunny belly, and lightest shells on tail, upper back, and face edge.

5. Continue mosaic in random application until complete; set aside to dry.

6. Using cuticle scissors, trim away any shells hanging over edges. Sand rough edges with emery board.

7. Apply 2-3 coats of extra-thick glaze sealer; let dry completely.

A RABBIT
pick is at home in a potted plant. Be sure to keep eggshelled embellishments away from water, which can loosen the shells.

LEATHER LETTER CADDY

Materials

- Acrylic paint: black
- Brush: No. 6 flat sable
- Clear glaze spray finish
- Cuticle scissors
- Decoupage medium
- Eggs: 10
- Emery board
- Leather letter caddy
- Transfer decals

Instructions

1. Paint entire letter caddy black; set aside to dry.

2. Decoupage white, unpainted eggshells to caddy; set aside to dry completely.

3. Adhere transfer decals to eggshell mosaic.

4. Using cuticle scissors, trim away any shells hanging over edges. Sand rough edges with emery board.

5. Apply 2 coats of clear glaze spray finish; set aside to dry.

JUST ABOUT *any worn leather desk accessory can be updated with eggshells and decals.*

COLOR

the holidays with some fun decorations like (clockwise from top left) a foam heart for Valentine's Day, a Fourth of July flag, a pumpkin-themed garden pick, and a glass votive holder for just about any occasion.

Chapter 7

CELEBRATE THE HOLIDAYS

Holiday items abound. There's no need to look for the perfect item for a particular occasion, only for the perfect item to eggshell mosaic. Making an obvious holiday object more special is the goal. Have no preconceived notions when beginning the search. Some choices will be easy to make, like the wooden hanging flag. Others may take courage, like the glass vase. The projects in this chapter are about trying different surfaces and adapting the objects' design to the eggshell mosaic process. Remember, if an object's surface is not in good shape, or if it looks inexpensive or worn out, eggshells can give it an awe-inspiring facelift and add some interest and texture at the same time. Break some eggs and begin!

HOLIDAY PROJECTS
Valentine Heart, Patriotic Flag, Pumpkin Ornament, Glass Votive Holder

VALENTINE HEART

Materials

- Acrylic paint: dark green, dark red, light green, light red, pink
- Bamboo skewers
- Brushes: ½" bristle china, No. 6 flat sable
- Decoupage medium
- Eggs: 6
- Extra-thick glaze sealer
- Florist's wire
- Foam heart
- Ribbon

Instructions

1. Break 1 egg in half.
2. Paint 1½ eggs with light red dots using bamboo skewer.
3. Paint 1½ eggs with light green dots using bamboo skewer.
4. Paint 2 eggs with pink flowers with dark red center and light green leaves.
5. Paint 1 egg with larger dark red flowers and dark green leaves.
6. Paint back of heart with 2 coats of dark red paint; let dry completely.
7. Decoupage eggshells to front of heart in random application; let dry.
8. Apply 2-3 coats of extra-thick glaze sealer.
9. Insert florist's wire into back of heart to create hanger.
10. Tie ribbon to heart.

EGGSTRA HELP

WORKING WITH FOAM FORMS

When applying paint to foam, it may be necessary to apply at least 2 coats in order to get complete coverage. To create a hanger for this project, insert florist's wire into foam shape and twist into a loop.

FOAM FORMS *can be cut into different shapes, but be sure not to use floral foam—it's made to retain wetness, so eggshells will slide off.*

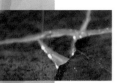

PATRIOTIC FLAG

Materials

- Acrylic paint: blue, red, white
- Brush: No. 6 flat sable
- Craft wire
- Cuticle scissors
- Decoupage medium
- Drill
- Eggs: 12
- Emery board
- Extra-thick glaze sealer
- Small wooden plaque
- String, raffia, or ribbon
- Wooden die cuts: letters U, S, and A

EGGSTRA HELP

WORKING WITH SEALERS

When working on projects with moving parts, try to keep both decoupage medium and sealer from getting between movable parts. If a project is going to be displayed outdoors, consider using a finishing product or sealer made for outdoor use.

Instructions

1. Drill small holes at top of each die cut letter and at bottom of plaque; attach letters to plaque with craft wire.

2. Drill 1 small hole at each top corner of plaque.

3. Paint 4 eggs red, 4 eggs blue, and leave 4 eggs unpainted.

4. Paint wooden project white on all sides.

5. Decoupage blue eggshells to front upper left section of plaque.

6. Beginning with red eggshells and on front only, decoupage first, third, and fifth stripes.

7. Decoupage unpainted shells to stripes two and four on flag front; let all shells dry.

8. With cuticle scissors, trim away any shells hanging over edges. Use emery board to sand rough edges.

9. Decoupage red eggshells to U, unpainted eggshells to S, and blue eggshells to A.

10. Trim and sand shells hanging over edges.

11. Apply 2-3 coats of extra-thick glaze sealer; let dry completely.

12. Attach string of choice to hang Patriotic Flag.

USE
decorative twine, ribbon, or raffia to hang your patriotic sign.

PUMPKIN ORNAMENT

Materials

- Acrylic paint: black, green, orange, yellow
- Brush: No. 6 flat sable
- Cuticle scissors
- Eggs: 2
- Emery board
- Extra-thick glaze sealer
- Wooden die cut: jack-o-lantern

Instructions

1. Break eggs into halves. Break 1 half into 2 quarters.
2. Paint front and back of die cut black.
3. Paint ½ egg orange.
4. Paint ½ egg orange and yellow blended.
5. Paint ½ egg orange and green blended.
6. Paint ¼ egg green, ¼ egg yellow.
7. Decoupage painted shells in random fashion, using yellow on teeth and green on stem.
8. With cuticle scissors, trim away any eggshells hanging over edges. Sand rough edges with emery board.
9. Apply 2 coats of extra-thick glaze sealer.

EGGSTRA HELP

BLENDING PAINT

This little project is more about blending a very few colors in the same family to create a textured look when painting eggshells. Different paint colors can be used on the same eggshell by blending edges where colors meet or by combining the two colors used together and painting an area between the two. By adding green to orange, a shade of brown is created; mixing yellow and orange creates a peach hue. There are no bad colors, only a color that is more comfortable in another space.

A WOODEN PUMPKIN, *turkey, or apple die cut can embellish a table arrangement or can be attached to a plain napkin ring for a festive holiday meal.*

GLASS VOTIVE HOLDER

Materials

- Acrylic paint: bright red, metallic copper, metallic gold, transparent pearl white

- Bamboo skewer

- Brush: No. 6 flat sable

- Decoupage medium

- Eggs: 9

- Extra-thick glaze sealer

- Paper towel

- Rubbing alcohol

- Tea light

- Votive holder

Instructions

1. Wipe surface of glass with rubbing alcohol to remove any fingerprints or oily spots.

2. Prime vase with glass primer or transparent pearl white acrylic paint; set aside to dry.

3. Paint 3 eggs bright red, 3 eggs metallic gold and metallic copper combined, and 3 eggs a combination of all colors.

4. Decoupage painted eggshells to one side of vase at a time, allowing that side to dry completely before moving on.

5. Apply 2 coats of extra-thick glaze sealer to entire vase; set aside to dry.

6. Place tea light at base of holder.

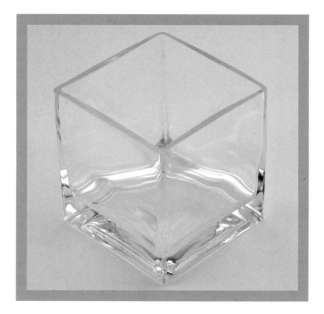

THINKING IN COLOR

The patterns on this page show how a black-and-white pattern (Diagram A) can be transformed into a colorful mosaic. You may like a particular design, but prefer to customize it to colors that suit your décor or personal taste. Every project in this book can be adapted. Use markers or colored pencils to fill in a pattern before you begin painting the eggshells and gluing. The image featured on page 123 was created with bolder hues, but equally stunning color combinations can be chosen (Diagrams B, C, and D).

Diagram A

Diagram B   *Diagram C*   *Diagram D*

Alternate Patterns

Just about any theme or color palette can be adapted to the eggshell mosaic projects featured throughout this book. If you love music, consider a musical instrument on your tabletop. If you enjoy floral designs you may like the patterns featured here. Enlarge and paint as desired.

ABOUT THE AUTHOR

At a very young age, Gail Dziuba enjoyed creating things. She was especially fond of sewing, crocheting, and knitting—just about anything that kept her hands busy and her mind free to roam. A Southerner tried and true, Gail studied art at Louisiana State University, never dreaming she would actually evolve into a professional artist nearly two decades later.

After her formal education, she married and dedicated her life to her family. When she reached her 40s, Gail bought a set of acrylics and picked up a paintbrush for the first time. It wasn't long before her art defined itself and she found herself experimenting with various mediums and materials—including eggshells.

Gail draws inspiration from the everyday—people, places, pastoral elements, and nature—and interprets these in a whimsical fashion. She takes a playful approach when painting scenes on furniture and people on canvas. Gail has illustrated a line of holiday cards entitled "Gaudy Claus," a tongue-in-cheek nod to her Texan neighbors. Her creative outlets are constantly developing just as she continues to grow as an artist.

In addition to eggshell mosaic projects, Gail has been hand painting furniture and wall murals for a number of years, in addition to many pieces of fine art.

She will never forget her high school art teacher, who happened to be challenged with a visual impairment. From her, Gail learned that nothing had to be perfect. And in art, she believes, this couldn't be more true.

Gail resides outside of Dallas, Texas with her husband, Dan.

CREDITS

Red Lips 4 Courage Communications Inc.
Book Editor: Catherine Risling
Photographer: Thomas McConnell
Stylist: Rebecca Ittner

Decoupage Medium

Mod Podge by Plaid

Glazes

Aleene's Paper Glaze

Krylon Triple Thick Crystal Clear Glaze

Glue

Aleene's Original Tacky Glue

Paint

Aleene's Premium-Coat acrylic craft paint

Americana Acrylic Paint by DecoArt

Anita's All-Purpose Acrylic Craft Paint

Apple Barrel Colors Acrylic Craft Paint
by Plaid

Delta Ceramcoat Acrylic Paint

FolkArt Acrylic Paint by Plaid

FolkArt Papier dimensional paint by Plaid

Sealer

FolkArt Clearcote Acrylic Sealer by Plaid

ACKNOWLEDGEMENTS

A special thanks to Emma, Chip, David, and Jeff Sanches, the Twisted Sisters, and Bill, Kevin, and Anna at Trinity District Antiques.

Metric Equivalency Charts

inches to millimeters and centimeters								yards to meters												
inches	mm	cm	inches	cm	inches	cm	yards	meters	yards	meters	yards	meters	yards	meters	yards	meters
1/8	3	0.3	9	22.9	30	76.2	1/8	0.11	2 1/8	1.94	4 1/8	3.77	6 1/8	5.60	8 1/8	7.43
1/4	6	0.6	10	25.4	31	78.7	1/8	0.11	2 1/8	1.94	4 1/8	3.77	6 1/8	5.60	8 1/8	7.43
1/2	13	1.3	12	30.5	33	83.8	1/4	0.23	2 1/4	2.06	4 1/4	3.89	6 1/4	5.72	8 1/4	7.54
5/8	16	1.6	13	33.0	34	86.4	3/8	0.34	2 3/8	2.17	4 3/8	4.00	6 3/8	5.83	8 3/8	7.66
3/4	19	1.9	14	35.6	35	88.9	5/8	0.46	2 1/2	2.29	4 1/2	4.11	6 1/2	5.94	8 1/2	7.77
7/8	22	2.2	15	38.1	36	91.4	5/8	0.57	2 5/8	2.40	4 5/8	4.23	6 5/8	6.06	8 5/8	7.89
1	25	2.5	16	40.6	37	94.0	3/4	0.69	2 3/4	2.51	4 3/4	4.34	6 3/4	6.17	8 3/4	8.00
1 1/4	32	3.2	17	43.2	38	96.5	7/8	0.80	2 7/8	2.63	4 7/8	4.46	6 7/8	6.29	8 7/8	8.12
1 1/2	38	3.8	18	45.7	39	99.1	1	0.91	3	2.74	5	4.57	7	6.40	9	8.23
1 3/4	44	4.4	19	48.3	40	101.6	1 1/4	1.03	3 1/4	2.86	5 1/8	4.69	7 1/4	6.52	9 1/8	8.34
2	51	5.1	20	50.8	41	104.1	1 1/4	1.14	3 1/4	2.97	5 1/4	4.80	7 1/4	6.63	9 1/4	8.46
2 1/2	64	6.4	21	53.3	42	106.7	1 3/8	1.26	3 3/8	3.09	5 3/8	4.91	7 3/8	6.74	9 3/8	8.57
3	76	7.6	22	55.9	43	109.2	1 1/2	1.37	3 1/2	3.20	5 1/2	5.03	7 1/2	6.86	9 1/2	8.69
3 1/2	89	8.9	23	58.4	44	111.8	1 5/8	1.49	3 5/8	3.31	5 5/8	5.14	7 5/8	6.97	9 5/8	8.80
4	102	10.2	24	61.0	45	114.3	1 3/4	1.60	3 3/4	3.43	5 3/4	5.26	7 3/4	7.09	9 3/4	8.92
4 1/2	114	11.4	25	63.5	46	116.8	1 7/8	1.71	3 7/8	3.54	5 7/8	5.37	7 7/8	7.20	9 7/8	9.03
5	127	12.7	26	66.0	47	119.4	2	1.83	4	3.66	6	5.49	8	7.32	10	9.14
6	152	15.2	27	68.6	48	121.9										
7	178	17.8	28	71.1	49	124.5										
8	203	20.3	29	73.7	50	127.0										

INDEX